W9-AGD-028

POWERING UP A CAREER IN BIOTECHNOLOGY

ERIC MINTON

ROSEN
PUBLISHING®

New York

Published in 2016 by The Rosen Publishing Group, Inc.
29 East 21st Street, New York, NY 10010

Copyright © 2016 by The Rosen Publishing Group, Inc.

First Edition

Library of Congress Cataloging-in-Publication Data

Minton, Eric, author.
Powering up a career in biotechnology/Eric Minton.—First edition.
    pages cm.—(Preparing for tomorrow's careers)
Includes bibliographical references and index.
ISBN 978-1-4994-6091-9 (library bound)
1. Biotechnologists—Juvenile literature. 2. Biotechnology—Vocational guidance—Juvenile literature. I. Title.
TP248.218.M56 2016
660.6023—dc23

                                                          2014044518

Manufactured in the United States of America

CONTENTS

INTRODUCTION

Vanessa Borcherding works as technology manager at the Institute for Computational Biomedicine at Weill Cornell Medical College. There, she's surrounded by life and machines in equal measure. Geneticists move DNA samples from temperature-controlled storage units to quarter-million-dollar high-throughput sequencers—humming white devices the size of a small refrigerator. That's where her work begins; each sequencer churns out up to three terabytes of data per week for the department's bioinformaticians to analyze.

When not upgrading her chilly server room—"Storage rates double every seven months," she says, "and they've increased a thousandfold over the past eight years"—Borcherding works on the institute's other devices, such as the Weill Cornell Visualization Facility, a two-million-dollar, state-of-the-art, viewer-controlled 3D virtual environment for examining everything from parts of a

A South African biotechnologist examines a food sample for *E. coli* bacteria. Biotech often involves hands-on work growing and studying living organisms in laboratories.

patient's brain to the structure of individual cells. "I get paid to play with cool toys," she says.

Biotechnology uses the tools and procedures of biology and biochemistry for scientific and industrial purposes. This includes everything from antibiotics and artificial sweeteners to waste treatment plants and X-ray machines. The term is new, the idea as old as civilization. When early humans first domesticated plants and animals for crops and livestock, or fermented foodstuffs to make cheese or beer, that was biotechnology.

Science and technology have evolved; so, too, has biotechnology. Germ theory resulted in the development of vaccination. Once drawn directly from infected humans or animals, vaccines are now manufactured in industrial quantities and save millions of lives each year. Food preservation has gone from salting and smoking to modern canning, flash-freezing, and pasteurization. Now foods that once rotted in days are safely eaten years later. In vitro fertilization and other fertility treatments allow infertile couples to bear children.

Because it touches on so many fast-moving scientific disciplines, biotechnology is ideally suited for go-getters who are always interested in learning more and finding new questions to answer.

Experienced, knowledgeable biotechnologists rarely lack for full-time employment or opportunities to share their knowledge with others. Experts may receive an annual travel budget in the tens of thousands of dollars to visit international conferences to learn more about the biological sciences, where they may be paid just to talk about their work.

CHAPTER ONE

NEW FRONTIERS IN BIOTECHNOLOGY

B iotechnology is an enormous field, touching on many other disciplines—biology, chemistry, engineering, even computer science and mathematics. Some noteworthy branches include:

- Bioinformatics—the study of biological and biochemical information. Genetic assays, protein folding studies, and other biotechnology projects generate masses of data that must be organized, stored, analyzed, and made understandable to scientists and engineers.
- Biomedical engineering—designing machines and processes to improve health care. These include diagnostic equipment, medical implants, and prosthetic limbs.
- Genetic engineering—the analysis and deliberate modification of genes in the laboratory. This includes modifying microorganisms so they'll create medicines, enhance the yield of crops, and treat disease by altering human DNA.
- Immunology—the study of the immune system. This includes strengthening it against disease and preventing it from attacking healthy tissues,

allergens, and useful foreign objects like transplanted organs or medical implants.

- Industrial biotechnology—using biotechnology in industrial settings. This includes food processing, manufacturing biofuels and bioplastics, and decontaminating industrial waste so it doesn't harm the environment.
- Microbiology—the study of microorganisms. Known for their role in studying pathogens to fight disease, microbiologists also work with beneficial microscopic creatures, like the nitrogen-fixing soil bacteria that allow crops to thrive or the yeasts used in making beer.

HOW BIOTECHNOLOGY HAS IMPROVED YOUR LIFE

Modern biotechnology touches every corner of the health care industry. This includes the vaccines you received as a child to protect against once-common diseases like measles and tetanus, the antibiotics your doctor prescribes when you're sick, and the X-ray machine your dentist uses to check your teeth for cavities. Synthetic insulin, an essential therapy for some forms of diabetes, comes from genetically modified bacteria. As you age, you may avail yourself of other medical advances, ranging from artificial pacemakers for heart conditions to cyclotrons that blast tumors with proton beams or X-rays

Genetically modified organisms are all the rage in food science debates, but almost everything you eat and drink involves biotechnology. Selective breeding makes farm animals larger and meatier than their predecessors. It also enhances size, sweetness, and juiciness of fruits and vegetables. Processed foods are enriched with vitamins, sweeteners, and colorants brewed up in factories, while many "natural" foods are genetically altered to be richer in vitamins and other nutrients. Fertilizers, livestock antibiotics, and pesticides improve agricultural yields. Crops are engineered to resist blights and pests.

This teen uses insulin injections to control her diabetes. Synthetic insulin was first produced in 1963. It became widely available in the 1980s.

Biotechnology also supports non-food-related industries. Fermentation or chemical processes turn corn into plastics and sewage into natural gas. Specialized bacteria extract metals like gold or uranium from low-quality ore. We use enzymes from animals or microbes to manufacture household goods like paper, leather, and textiles with little chemical waste. Enzymes also clean contact lenses and improve detergents' stain-fighting ability.

ADVANCES IN GENETIC ENGINEERING

Geneticists continue tweaking the genes of living things to give them new traits. Transgenic cats, pigs, and rabbits are born with DNA from bioluminescent jellyfish, making them glow in the dark. Silkworms with spider genes produce stronger silk. Some poplar trees have been engineered to soak up thirty times as much of the pollutant tri-chloroethylene as a normal tree. Others were modified to break down more easily in the papermaking process, reducing energy costs and pollution.

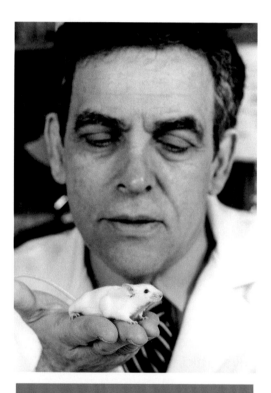

In this 1998 photo, Dr. Philip Leder of Harvard Medical School holds the first transgenic mouse to be granted a patent by the U.S. patent office.

Salmon altered to produce more growth hormone grew twice as fast as ordinary salmon. Bananas modified to include the genes for vaccines will vaccinate people who eat them. Engineered cows produce milk resembling human breast milk, increasing its nutritional value while removing proteins to which some babies are allergic.

CLONING

Cloning, or engineering a new organism to be genetically identical to an existing one, has had some success over the years. Since Dolly the cloned sheep's birth in 1996, mice, goats, pigs, and cattle have been cloned. Now, cloning techniques produce copies of human embryonic stem cells—which have the potential to be used to treat any number of diseases—to match a donor's genetic code, preventing tissue rejection. These are created by implanting body tissue from the patient into an unfertilized human ovum, one from which the nucleus has generally been removed. One patient's severed spinal cord, a seemingly permanent injury, was healed using nasal cavity cells as a "scaffold" to support and nurture a nerve cell graft.

ADVANCES IN BIOMEDICAL ENGINEERING

Countless advanced medical devices are under development today. For example, biochemists and biomedical engineers hope to diagnose hundreds of health problems simply by scanning a patient's breath with lasers to measure chemicals related to various health conditions, like ammonia for kidney failure and acetone for diabetes.

Surgery is more sophisticated than ever. Brain surgery may no longer need to open the skull; a curved, segmented needle can enter through the cheek, its path guided using a magnetic resonance imaging (MRI) scanner. Eye-surgery devices increase precision for delicate operations while filtering out tremors or other irrelevant movements in the surgeon's hands. "Force feedback" systems allow surgeons to experience tactile feedback when using surgical robots, effectively "feeling" what the mechanisms touch.

Surgical implants have come a long way since early bone-repair pins and screws. New technologies include pain blockers that shut down the nerves responsible for chronic pain and lenses implanted into eyes to counteract age-related vision problems. Biodegradable plastic bone grafts are used to give shape and structure to stem cells that grow on the plastic framework to form new bones. Three-dimensional printing is poised to bring us "printed organs," laying down cultured cells to form everything from skin to livers.

Some devices interact directly with the higher nervous system. Retinal implants transmit signals from a camera to the brain, restoring sight to the blind. With brain-machine interfaces, paralyzed people will directly control robotic artificial limbs. New brain-scanning techniques can determine if someone in a coma is unconscious, or aware of their surroundings but unable to communicate.

All these advancements are the work of scientists, engineers, and technicians involved with biotechnology. But for all the resources available to researchers, progress

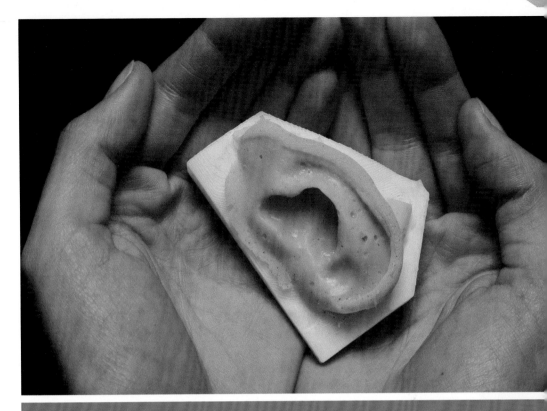

Three-dimensional printing technology is approaching the point at which organs such as ears can be built from human cells and grafted onto a patient's body instead of scarce donor organs.

is slow and intermittent. Government regulations surround research and development, preventing release of new technologies until they're thoroughly tested in clinical trials to ensure they're safe and effective—a process that takes years, during which private industries make no profit and can indeed go out of business.

CHAPTER TWO

EDUCATION–
SEQUENCING YOUR
FUTURE

Your road to a biotech career starts with high-school coursework. No matter which field you end up specializing in, you'll want a solid grounding in STEM—science, technology, engineering, and mathematics—courses. Let's examine the nuts and bolts of a biotech-oriented education plan.

DECODING THE SCIENCES

Though biology is the heart of biotechnology, it isn't the only relevant field. Living things are made of matter, so you'll want a solid grounding in chemistry to properly understand biology and biochemistry. But while biology and chemistry are the most relevant sciences to study for a biotech career, any class or extracurricular activity in the sciences, from physics to psychology, will help you. All sciences rely on the scientific method—the structured way in which researchers study problems, propose hypotheses, and test them with experiments. Broader knowledge of the sciences can only help in your future career, as you don't know what specialization you'll end up in. After all, the only way to know what branch of the biological sciences you'll most enjoy is to study

Students interested in biotechnology have several ways to get directly involved, including school lab work, after-school clubs, competitions, and internships at university laboratories.

as many subjects as you can. Indeed, you may find that instead of biotechnology, your real passion lies elsewhere.

Mathematics is also important. It's a "gatekeeper subject." No matter whether you focus on biochemistry, genetics, computer science, or engineering, you'll need to excel in math. Statistics is fundamental to analyzing genetic data, as without it you'll be lost in a morass of indecipherable assay results. In molecular biology, you need algebra to calculate the concentrations of molecules inside of cells and calculus to model rates of population growth.

Computer science will also serve you well in many biotech fields, particularly bioinformatics. Computer programs are the tools you'll use to apply your math skills to many problems, especially to analyze lab data. In engineering, you'll use computerized drafting programs to design new biotech devices and both hardware and software skills to build those devices' microprocessors. You don't need to study a specific programming language—there are no standards in the field—but the more languages you know, the easier it is to pick up new ones. Practice studying the ins and outs of computer programs you use; this is a valuable habit when learning to use new programs on the job.

Aim for advanced placement classes when possible. They'll push you toward advanced skills that will come in handy in college. An easy A in a non-AP class may improve your grade point average, but it won't improve your skill set.

SKILLS, NOT COURSES

More important than the specific courses you take are the skills you learn. Critical thinking is essential; scientists must examine data with an open mind and draw conclusions without prejudgment. This comes from learning and internalizing the scientific method. Only with experience—acquired in the lab as a working professional or from school science experiments—can you learn to ask the right questions and discard irrelevant information. Experts in the field recommend studying *Bloom's Taxonomy* to learn more about critical thinking to develop your analytical skills further.

Presentation is an important skill for anyone working in the sciences. In-depth knowledge, a keen eye for hypotheses, diligent and accurate lab work—none of these help your career if you can't persuade employers, supervisors, or peers to give you and your ideas a chance. Beyond that, communication skills are important for teaching classes, training colleagues, making presentations at conferences, and acing job interviews. Communications and English classes will help, as will

Communication is critical for scientists and technicians. They share information, offer progress reports to managers or senior scientists, and make presentations before their peers at conferences.

a stint on the debate team. Learn to use presentation software like Microsoft PowerPoint to make your case colorfully and succinctly.

Beyond subject matter and skills, the most important thing you'll need to pursue a career in biotech is dedication. Talent takes you only so far. You'll need to try things you have no experience with and push yourself to give your all. Don't be afraid of failure; that's how you learn. Success comes from hard work, not innate intelligence.

This will be particularly important once you're out of school and on the job, where you'll have to educate yourself further in whatever field you're working in. Project leaders are often too busy with their own research—and writing grants to obtain funding for their work—to personally train graduate students or newly fledged researchers and technicians. You'll have to figure things out on your own.

EXTRACURRICULARS

In addition to classwork, you'll benefit from independent exposure to the biological sciences. Here are several valuable potential sources for independent study:

- Reading books and websites on your own time, rather than as part of your coursework. Research your sources; anything more than a few years old is out-of-date, and many educational resources have a pro- or anti-biotech agenda.
- Online participatory "citizen science" projects. Also known as crowd-sourced science, this is

online research—often gamelike—performed by large numbers of amateurs, from middle school students to retirees. Examples include Foldit, designed to develop new proteins for medical and other uses; EteRNA, where players design RNA molecules to help develop faster and better algorithms for genetic modeling; and Zooniverse, a platform hosting a wide range of citizen science projects.

- School clubs and after-school projects. If your school has no extracurricular programs in the life sciences, you or your parents can speak to the principal or other high-ranking school staff about starting such a program. (Getting involved in starting or running an after-school program will also provide valuable leadership experience.)
- Biotech competitions. There are several contests every year—some regional and some national—that award prizes to individuals or teams for innovative biotech research. Some are open to high school students.
- Mentorship. Spend as much time as you can with good teachers so you can learn from them outside the classroom as well.
- Some local colleges and universities have outreach programs to educate younger students about the life sciences. However, you or your teachers may need to make the first move to make things happen. "It helps when a teacher reaches out to a scientist with a lesson plan for a specific class," says Elizabeth Waters, Ph.D., lead scientist at the Rockefeller University Science Outreach Program.

- You can connect with an appropriate department—biotechnology, biology, biochemistry, etc.—of a local college or university and ask to help in the lab. But make sure you know enough about the field that you have more to offer than a pair of hands. "Have an idea you'd like to test or a question to answer," Waters says. "Do the thinking first."

HIGHER EDUCATION

Majors in biotechnology and noteworthy subfields, like bioinformatics or biomedical engineering, are becoming more common. But not every college has a dedicated biotechnology department, nor is every life sciences department a top-notch program. When choosing a college, do your research. Admissions departments will tell you what majors and courses are available, but there's lots of other information that you'll want to search for elsewhere. This includes an institution's reputation among employers, the quality of its educators (both as scientists and as teachers), the ratio of students to faculty, the funding available to its life sciences department, and availability of financial aid.

Ivy League schools and other big-name institutions are very expensive. Before committing to such a school, research salaries in your chosen field and compare them to your expected student loan payments to get a sense of what your financial situation will look like at various points during your career. While having a Harvard or CalTech degree on your résumé looks good to hiring managers, it may not be worth

A doctoral candidate and two students use enzymes to break down organic compounds at the Institute of Technical Biocatalysis, at Hamburg University of Technology, in Germany.

the expense, especially when employers recognize the quality of a program at a less expensive school. On the other hand, highly competitive schools sometimes offer more generous financial aid packages.

While you can enter some lab technician careers with an associate's degree, most biotech careers require at least a bachelor's degree. Advanced research or teaching positions may call for a master's or doctorate. Consider

CASH TRANSFUSIONS

College is far more expensive today than a generation ago. Even at public universities, four years of tuition, housing, and food costs close to $100,000. Private universities average twice that. And these expenses are increasing; by 2040, a college education may run to nearly $300,000.

You'll want to look into additional sources of financial aid to pay for tuition, including student loans, scholarships, grants, and work-study programs. These can come from a number of sources—the federal government, your state government, your college, or private organizations. You'll have to research sources of financial aid, but there are resources available to help you, including:

- **The U.S. Department of Education's Office of Federal Student Aid (accessible at https://studentaid.ed.gov) or the government of Canada's Student Loans Program (at http://www.canlearn.ca/eng/loans _grants/index.shtml).**
- **Your state or province's grant agency.**
- **The college's financial aid office and your major's department, both of which can help you find scholarships and grants related to your field of study.**

a bachelor's if you and your family can afford it, to gain access to a wider range of job offers. Postgraduate education takes so much money and time—time you could invest in the workplace to earn money and experience—that you should carefully consider whether it's worthwhile, either for a specific career's requirements or because you really want to pursue higher learning for its own sake.

Not every career path demands an early focus on that career. Engineering jobs require engineering

Students can work directly with scientists and gain hands-on experience with biotechnology by volunteering at a university lab or obtaining an internship at a biotech company.

degrees, but you can make it in bioinformatics with something as divergent as a psychology degree. Do some research beforehand to figure out how much flexibility you have in your choice of major—or whether you need to carve your major in stone during your freshman year.

Whatever your major, take a variety of courses rather than focusing too narrowly on a chosen specialty. Without new experiences, you can't be sure where your talents and interests lie in the long term. Even if your first biochemistry or genomics course really excites you, you may find something else that attracts you even more. A broad range of skills and aptitudes will benefit you no matter what your major or your career.

CHAPTER THREE

GENES AND CELLS– LABORATORY CAREERS

Scientific research is the beating heart of biotechnology. All the exotic drugs and devices manufactured by the biotech industry are made possible by researchers testing hypotheses in the lab. Research contributes to a wide range of interrelated fields, including genomics, microbiology, molecular biology, and biochemistry.

Before we begin, let's distinguish between basic and applied research. Basic research aims solely at expanding scientific knowledge, so we better understand the principles by which the natural world functions. This research rarely yields information usable to design marketable products, so for-profit companies see it a losing proposition. Instead, basic research receives funding from national and regional governments, universities, and nonprofit groups.

Applied research is aimed at solving specific real-world problems and developing useful or desirable products, such as creating vaccines for previously untreatable diseases or formulating better biodegradable plastics. Work in applied research is often for private industry.

BIOCHEMISTRY

Biochemists research chemical processes related to biological processes and living beings, such as cell reproduction and growth, enzymatic action, and genetics. They perform both basic and applied research, studying organic chemicals such as allergens, biofuels, enzymes, and pharmaceuticals, and analyzing the effects of various substances on living cells, tissues, and metabolism.

Subject matter of biochemical research ranges from medical and pharmaceutical research and testing—such as investigating new approaches to fight cancer—to agriculture and food processing, manufacturing, and waste purification. Anything involving organic compounds or biological action is in biochemists' wheelhouse.

Biochemical research is full-time work, where it's often necessary to put in extra-long hours. Biochemists spend much of their time in laboratories working with all sorts of technological devices, such as high-powered lasers for chemical analysis. They may need to work with dangerous substances or contagious microorganisms, requiring protective gear and strict safety procedures. They often work in teams, either with other biochemists or with experts in other fields, such as biochemical engineers or bioinformaticians.

Unlike many biotechnology job paths, a research biochemist career generally requires a doctorate. This can build off a bachelor's degree in any number of related fields, such as biology, chemistry, engineering, or physics. Math and computer science are also critical

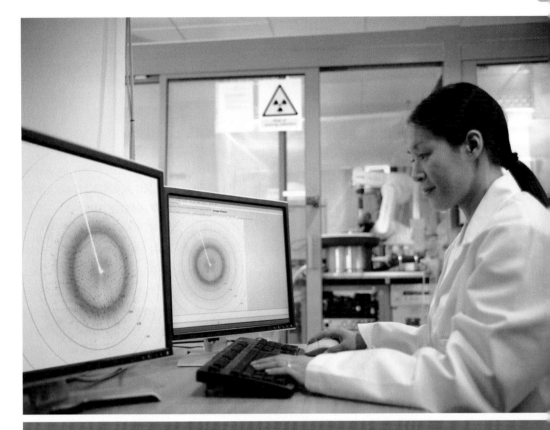

A biochemist studies X-ray results from a protein sample frozen in liquid nitrogen. Biotechnology labs employ a range of sophisticated tools for analyzing and modifying biological materials.

for analyzing the results of biochemistry experiments. Additional lab experience is valuable and can be gained in university labs or through corporate internships.

Writing is an important skill for biochemists—or anyone else working in academic research—as advancing your career requires publishing your results in academic journals. Management skills are also important, as project leaders spend much of their time supervising subordinates and writing grant proposals.

BIOINFORMATICS

Bioinformaticians use databases and computer programs to gather, store, organize, and model biological data. Perhaps the most active and exciting branch of bioinformatics is genomics. Geneticists study and modify genes. Genes are the DNA sequences that cells use as a blueprint to build proteins. They are passed along when

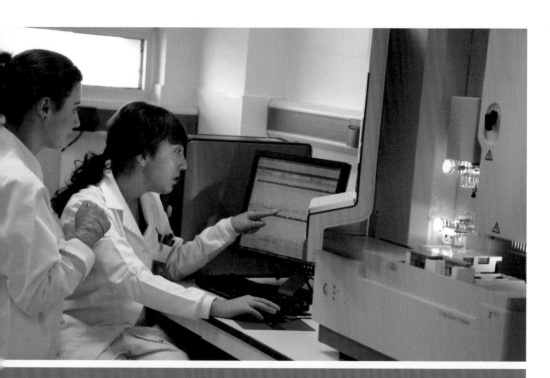

Two bioinformaticians work with an automatic gene sequencer and study the results. Computer science skills are invaluable for sorting through the masses of data generated in the laboratory.

cells divide. New organisms are created when DNA from one partner mixes with DNA from the other during sexual reproduction. Researchers have cataloged the entire genetic sequence of dozens of organisms, including the human genome. By determining the functions of various genes, both independently and in concert with others, geneticists play an important role in fighting disease and in modifying various living creatures—from microorganisms to livestock—to better serve humanity.

Other bioinformatics subfields deal with non-genetic molecular data. Proteomics deals with protein engineering, for example, while cheminformatics deals with pharmaceutical design. Non-genetic bioinformatics requires the ability to search databases quickly for molecules with similar structures or effects to a target molecule—something that's very tricky to code.

While Linux is the most commonly used operating system in bioinformatics, each research facility uses different programming languages and software. Bioinformaticians need to be flexible, using whatever databases, statistical modeling, or graphic modeling software is on hand. The more languages and programs you study now, the easier you'll find it to pick up new ones quickly.

Given the constant need to devise and improve sorting algorithms, and to find clear ways of modeling mountains of data, bioinformaticians need a strong grasp of mathematics. A solid understanding of statistics is essential. Calculus is also useful.

Bioinformaticians typically work full-time. It's a growing field, full of potential for workers knowledgeable in both computer science and the life sciences. As genetic

PERRSONALIZED MEDICINE

Medicine isn't as simple as diagnosing a disease or disorder and prescribing a remedy. Everyone's body works slightly differently. We each have allergies, resistances, and sensitivities to various medications and treatments. A physician has to take these things into account when treating patients. Much of treatment is trial and error—figuring out what drugs or procedures will best help a patient and in what doses, while minimizing negative side effects.

Our unique reactions to treatment are decided, in large part, by our genes. Genetic researchers investigate and identify interactions between our genes and our reactions to medication. The end goal is personalized medicine—a way to bypass all that trial and error by reading a patient's genetic profile and using it to learn exactly what treatment to administer for any given medical problem.

assaying becomes cheaper and faster, bioinformaticians have more and more data to manage. Opportunities should also open up for cybersecurity experts as the field becomes more lucrative.

A doctorate isn't necessary for a bioinformatics job, and many workers in the field have only limited computer science experience. Still, an advanced degree is useful to obtain a high-end position. More important is a broad range of related skills, as well as the ability to learn and master new computer programs and languages quickly.

Several universities offer certification in bioinformatics. This typically requires only a few classes. Even if you don't go into bioinformatics, the skills learned in those classes are useful in a biotechnology career and certification is valuable for job placement.

BIOLOGICAL TECHNICIANS

Biological technicians work with and support biochemists, geneticists, and other biological scientists. Though they're grounded in the same sciences as the researchers they collaborate with, technicians focus on practical work rather than ideas. In addition to a range of practical tasks—preparing and cleaning lab equipment, collecting and preparing samples for analysis, writing reports—they use the same facilities and tools as the scientists they support, working with everything from gene sequences to robot arms. Gathering specimens can take them out of the lab, whether to obtain marine life at sea or to harvest fungi from the forest floor.

Biological technicians work in teams under the supervision of researchers or engineers. However, they can work their way up the ladder—not only to take on more technical responsibilities but also to hold research roles. In addition, experienced technicians provide valuable institutional knowledge by training and teaching less-experienced researchers who are new to the

Biological technicians need to have excellent observational and analytical skills. They need to be precise and thorough, too.

team. Most biological technicians work full-time, but they can leave work at the door. In 2012, 20 percent of biological technicians worked part-time.

Working as a technician requires a methodical approach. You'll use advanced equipment that requires precise handling, and you'll need keen, alert senses to make accurate observations of experiments in progress. Working with scientists also requires good communication skills to ensure that you're always on the same page regarding instructions and that you report your results clearly and concisely.

You'll want a bachelor's degree in biology or a similar field to find employment as a biological technician. A couple of years of lab experience—whether from lab courses or from extracurricular collaboration with faculty members—is also valuable. So is specialization in a specific field, such as microbiology or physiology.

CHAPTER FOUR

LIFE'S BUILDING BLOCKS–INDUSTRIAL CAREERS

T here is no dividing line between science and engineering," says Doug Darr, Ph.D., vice president of business development at food research organization Nutrasearch and former biotechnology instructor at Piedmont Community College. "The tools are different, but the methods are the same."

The industrial side of the biotechnology industry covers the actual design and manufacture of health and consumer products, such as drugs, fertilizers, and processed foods. It's a lot more hands-on than pure research, and you'll be working more in factories than laboratories. But the work is just as tough, and the science just as rigorous.

BIOCHEMICAL ENGINEERING

Biochemical engineers find real-world industrial applications for the life sciences, translating formulas and principles developed by scientists in the lab into full-scale manufacturing processes.

33

A biological engineer at a Portland, Maine, sewage treatment plant is applying indigo solution to water samples to test for contamination.

Unlike the inorganic materials involved in conventional engineering, biological engineering works with living organisms, either directly or indirectly. This covers a range of industries, such as agriculture, biodegradable products, biofuels, food processing, and waste purification and recycling. Responsibilities include designing tools and processes; determining how best to lay out equipment; testing and monitoring bioreactors and other manufacturing facilities to ensure that processes run as planned; and designing safety procedures and ensuring that they're adhered to in the workplace.

Biological and biochemical expertise have a major role in chemical production. Engineers use fermentation and enzymatic processes to transform organic materials, creating substances like vitamins, high fructose corn syrup, insulin, ethanol, and plastics. As beer is the result of fermentation, large breweries hire biochemical engineers (not to mention

This oenologist—a wine-making scientist—in Barcelona, Spain, is taking a sample of red wine from a large fermentation tank to examine its properties and quality.

microbiologists) to manage the brewing process and fine-tune it for quality and flavor.

To work in the field, you'll want a bachelor's degree in biochemical engineering from a U.S. university accredited by ABET (formerly known as the Accreditation Board for Engineering and Technology), or from a Canadian university accredited by the Canadian Engineering Accreditation Board. Alternatively, you can start with an accredited bachelor's in another engineering field and then get a master's degree or work experience in bio-chemical engineering.

Accreditation is important because you need an accredited degree (along with multiple years of experience and passing two examinations) to earn a professional engineer license in your state. Licensing is legally required to perform certain duties, limiting your ability to move up in the field without it. Not every school's programs are accredited; visit the ABET website's Accredited Program Search page to see which colleges will provide accredited courses.

CROSS-CUTTING PRINCIPLES

Specializing in a single field—learning all there is to know about one subject—sounds like a winning formula for a successful career. But that's not the case, according to biotechnology professionals. Instead, it's important to dedicate yourself to multiple fields of study.

No matter how much you know about your chosen field, you'll face competition from others following the same career path. You also may not have as much to offer as someone else in the field with more talent, education, or experience. Broadening your skill set by learning about biotechnology topics outside of your specialty adds value for potential employers.

You'll get a lot of useful experience out of lab work and field study. (Also, employers value work experience, internships, and other practical hands-on training.) Some research positions call for a graduate degree. Continuing education is important to keep up with advances in both biochemistry and engineering.

High school preparation for a biochemical engineering career involves a full range of science courses—biology, chemistry, physics—as well as a solid grounding in math, from algebra and geometry to trigonometry and calculus. You'll also need good writing and

More important, studying additional fields gives you insight into problems that touch on those fields. Learning more about microbiology, for instance, helps agricultural engineers work with microbial issues such as nitrogen fixing or crop blights. This even applies to non-biotechnology fields, such as psychology's relevance to studies of the brain.

Like any scientific discipline, biotechnology is split into a bewildering array of subfields and sub-subfields. You may end up working in biomimetics, synthetic biology, pharmacogenetics, or bioprocess engineering. Ultimately, the distinction is based on what you do and how you do it, not what you know—and certainly not who you are.

communication skills, as you'll be working with other engineers, scientists, and technicians to set up procedures, make sure they're followed, and troubleshoot problems.

Biochemical engineering is a full-time job. You may work in a research lab or at manufacturing plants, refineries, and other private industrial sites. This can involve lots of travel!

AGRICULTURAL AND FOOD SCIENCE

These agricultural scientists are studying banana plants in a greenhouse. The field can involve long hours of hands-on activity at agricultural sites.

Agricultural scientists bring biotechnology to the farm. Agriculture and aquaculture involve herbicides and pesticides, water aeration, and soil chemistry. These scientists study plant and animal genetics to hybridize strains for any number of desirable qualities— crop yields, nutritional value, appearance, texture and flavor, and the ability to withstand travel and storage. They're also

CHARTING THE BIOTECH SECTOR

While big biotechnology companies like Genentech get their share of media attention, they're not the only places looking to hire biotech specialists. Many industries—from food processing to biofuels and from pharmaceuticals to cosmetics—value biotechnology experts.

In addition, there's room for biotechnologists in the public sector. Some government agencies—including the armed forces—perform basic and applied research, while others, like the U.S. Food and Drug Administration, are responsible for overseeing industries involved in biotech research and development. Universities need skilled teachers and researchers in their life sciences and engineering departments, too, of course.

involved with other aspects of food processing, such as packaging and food preservation.

Agricultural scientists do most of their work in labs and offices, and they typically have standard full-time working hours. But their responsibilities may take them to farms, fisheries, or food-processing plants, where they work in environments with extreme temperatures, loud noises, and exposure to potential biohazards, including animal blood and waste. This is not a career for the squeamish!

Work in the field requires at least an ABET-accredited bachelor's degree. Specific coursework varies widely based on what subfield of agricultural science you're working in; you may want to look at food chemistry, microbiology, genetics, botany, or even entomology (for pests). As usual, biology, chemistry, and math are your mainstays, and you'll want to focus on communication skills in order to explain procedures and results to coworkers outside your specialty. Getting an internship is recommended, as it provides valuable hands-on experience in the field.

Animal scientists typically have more advanced degrees than food, soil, or plant scientists. They may also choose to study veterinary medicine for more insight into animals; this requires a bachelor's degree.

Some states require a license, with requirements varying by state. In addition, several professional organizations, such as the American Registry of Professional Animal Scientists, the Institute of Food Technologists, and the Soil Science Society of America, offer certification for agricultural scientists. Certification isn't usually required to find work, but employers recognize its value.

CHAPTER FIVE

WE CAN REBUILD YOU–BIOMEDICINE CAREERS

The intersection between technology and medicine is broad and deep. All the tools of the physician's trade—from sphygmomanometers to syringes, scalpels to stethoscopes—are carefully engineered to fulfill their functions. Anesthetics and antibiotics alike are manufactured and tested by pharmaceutical engineers. Skilled technicians perform echocardiograms to look for heart disease and blood tests for any number of pathogens.

BIOMEDICAL ENGINEERING

Biomedical engineers apply biological and medical research to improve human health. They design practical solutions for medical problems in such forms as new medical procedures, software to operate medical equipment and run drug testing simulations, diagnostic devices, surgical implants, and prosthetics, all with the goal of saving lives and improving quality of life in a medical setting.

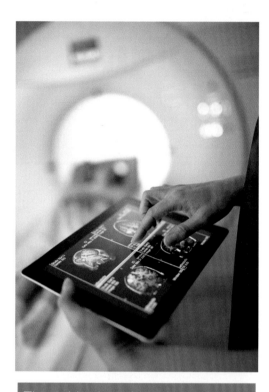

This tablet lets doctors view a patient's brain scan images in real time. Biomedical engineers develop this sort of cutting-edge technology.

Job environments vary a lot for biomedical engineers. They can perform research in the lab, test new mechanisms and procedures in hospitals, or work out assembly line issues in a factory. They collaborate with a range of other professionals, from scientists to doctors to factory managers and workers; this calls for good communication skills. While they typically work regular full-time hours, the needs of patients and clients may require overtime.

To work in the field, you'll want a bachelor's degree in biomedical engineering from an ABET-accredited U.S. university or a Canadian Engineering Accreditation Board–accredited Canadian university, or an accredited bachelor's in another engineering field followed by a master's degree or work experience in biomedical engineering. Going to medical school or dental school can also provide valuable knowledge of and experience with patient care.

In high school, you should study sciences like biology, chemistry, and physics, as well as computer science and mathematics, especially calculus. In addition, technical drawing—the craft of precisely depicting an object's construction and function—is an essential skill for engineers.

Employment in the biomedical engineering field is expected to grow in the coming years due to both the development of a range of more sophisticated tools and the increased medical needs of an aging population.

DO-IT-YOURSELF BIOTECHNOLOGY

Biotechnology labs are full of equipment that costs millions of dollars, with reagents that cost thousands of dollars per use. You may find carefully temperature-controlled shelves full of genetic samples and assaying chemicals, icy rooms packed with multi-petabyte disk arrays and high-end servers, or three-dimensional printers for constructing prototype medical devices.

You don't need all that stuff to learn about biotechnology, though. In addition to online citizen science projects, there are genetic experiments you can perform in your own home without an advanced lab full of

(continued on the next page)

(continued from the previous page)

cutting-edge gear. In fact, it's getting easier to do so every year. The cost of tools and reagents keeps dropping. Miniaturization turns gear that once filled buildings into items you can fit in your closet.

Biohackers—participants in the so-called biopunk movement—are dedicated to home-brew genetics and free access to genetic information. With a laptop, publicly available gene sequence data, mail-order synthetic DNA—available from sources like the BioBricks Foundation, or iGEM's Registry of Standard Biological Parts—and household chemicals, you can perform your own genetic experiments, from building glow-in-the-dark bacteria to examining your own DNA for genes related to family health problems.

While immensely educational if you're planning on pursuing a career in biotech, biohacking can be an expensive hobby. Even when bought secondhand through industry contacts or online, important devices such as an electrophoresis gel box or autoclave can cost hundreds or thousands of dollars. Even so, prices continue to drop every year. Affordable, publically accessible shared lab spaces, like San Francisco–area nonprofit BioCurious, are beginning to crop up. By the time you're sufficiently well-versed in biotechnology that you feel you actually need some of the more expensive devices, you should be sufficiently dedicated to the biotech career track to make the investment worthwhile.

MEDICAL LABORATORY SCIENCE

Medical laboratory scientists, technologists, and technicians investigate problems with patients' health by performing tests in hospitals and laboratories. They operate a variety of diagnostic devices, such as magnetic resonance imaging (MRI) systems and ultrasound transducers. They collect and analyze samples of bodily tissues, fluids, and other specimens. They discuss

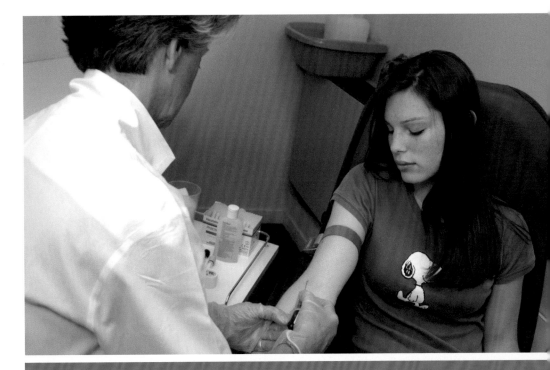

This hospital nurse is performing a phlebotomy—drawing blood—from a young patient. Blood samples are sent to laboratories to test for diseases and genetic disorders.

findings with patients' physicians. Technicians typically perform simpler or partially automated tasks under the direction of a medical laboratory scientist.

Medical laboratories vary in size. In small labs, technologists have to perform many duties and learn a wide range of skills and techniques. In larger labs, they specialize

Working in a medical laboratory involves collaborating with many other technologists and technicians.

in specific types of medical science, such as hematology (the study of blood-borne diseases), immunology, or genetic analysis.

If you want to become a technologist, you should aim to earn a bachelor's degree in medical laboratory technology—also called clinical laboratory science—although a bachelor's in another life sciences field will suffice if you've completed required courses in fields like biology and chemistry. Becoming a technician rather than a technologist requires only an associate's degree.

Some states require a professional license, and many employers prefer to hire licensed candidates. Be sure to pick a college with an accredited program that is accepted by the American Society for Clinical

THE EDGE OF THE BIOTECH UMBRELLA

Not everyone who works in biotechnology is a scientist, engineer, or technician. There are numerous tangentially related fields that provide opportunities to work for biotech companies and agencies. These include intellectual property law, drug marketing, or even teaching. Even if your temperament isn't well-suited to science and engineering, these provide options to get involved in the field.

Naturally, biotech companies also have employees that perform tasks found in any other industry, such as management, accounting, and human resources. As with the aforementioned job fields, some knowledge of the life sciences will stand you in good stead here. "A four-year life science degree is useful but not absolutely necessary," says Nutrasearch's Dr. Darr. "It gives you the background to deal with scientific questions without having to run to the company president for answers."

Even if you go into science or engineering, biotechnology employees offer an additional vector for networking. Not every professional contact in biotechnology works in the lab!

Pathology or the Canadian Society for Medical Laboratory Science.

High school coursework includes biology, chemistry, and math. You'll also need to have nimble hands, as you'll be working with very precise instruments—not to mention needles! Strength and endurance are likewise important, as you'll be on your feet all day and may need to physically move patients in order to perform tests or obtain samples. You'll also need to follow safety precautions for working with potentially infectious biological materials, such as sterilizing equipment and wearing protective clothing.

Biological medicine is full-time work. Some facilities—such as hospitals—are open around the clock, which provides opportunities for night owls.

CHAPTER SIX

RESEARCH AND DEVELOPMENT– PLANNING YOUR JOB SEARCH

Searching for a job is much the same in bio-technology as in any other field. Experts in many biotech careers are currently in high demand, but there's no way to tell how that will change between now and the time you enter the job market with your college degree in hand. You'll need to approach the job hunt with the same diligence and precision that you'll apply to the work itself.

THE EARLY BIRD GETS THE JOB

It's never too early to start thinking about a biotech job. Start networking while you're still in school. You can meet people with biotech connections both locally—by visiting local universities and bio-tech companies to discuss your ideas—and online. Share your contact information at career fairs. Stay on good terms with fellow students; friends are the most reliable professional contacts.

Biotech companies send recruiters to job fairs, like the Black Data Processing Associates career fair in Washington, D.C., shown here, to offer biotech workers employment.

Put together your first résumé and LinkedIn profile now. You can improve them over time. Figure out what your dream job is and start making connections there. Don't be afraid to ask for introductions from your contacts, even if you hardly know them. When the time comes for you to get a job at the company or university of your choice, you want to know as many people there as possible!

But remember that the industry isn't static. Your current dream company may be on the rocks financially by the time you graduate. Keep your options open, and research developments in the industry—such as the status of clinical trials—so you can predict which companies will be hiring new blood.

EVOLVING YOUR RÉSUMÉ

Start with a résumé that gives a good first impression. Ensure that it's well written, with no typos or grammatical errors, and that it concisely and accurately portrays your experience. Keep it short—no more than one page, especially if you're just out of college. Résumé writing is a field all its own, and you'll benefit from reading books on résumé writing and talking to experts such as human resources directors or trainers at your local unemployment office.

However, "your résumé" is a misnomer. You'll want to customize each résumé you send out so that it fits the needs and desires of the employer you're sending it to. Add keywords from the job description, and move your most relevant experience and education to the top of the résumé, while minimizing or removing irrelevant experience. This will both make it more engaging to a human reader and improve your odds of being picked out of the pile by automated résumé-hunting programs.

Even if you're fresh out of college, there's a lot of useful information you can put on your résumé. Include lab projects, work-study programs, awards, and certifications. Focus on

When working on your résumé, it helps to collaborate with teachers or fellow students to make sure that it is well-edited and properly formatted.

RUNNING IN PLACE JUST TO KEEP UP

High school classes and college courses will give you your start in biotechnology, but they're not enough. More so than most fields, biotech requires you to keep learning for the rest of your life.

Genetic and biochemical research is tied to computer speed and processing power, as researchers work with larger and more complicated masses of data to perform genetic assays and solve molecular folding problems. Computer processing power and data storage has roughly doubled every two years for decades now. This holds true in the lab as well, where high-throughput gene sequencers turn out terabytes of data every week.

As knowledge advances in biotechnology, workers must scramble to keep up. Scientists and engineers need to keep a close eye on new results at all times in order to remain up-to-date. "This is the fastest movement of technology in our lifetime," says Christopher Mason, Ph.D., assistant professor of computational and systems biomedicine at Weill Cornell Medical College. "The field moves so quickly that data from just five years ago is disastrously outdated today."

If you're interested in biotechnology, be prepared to constantly read and study advances in your field and related topics, and to keep studying long after you finish school. Biotech scientists may find little time for hobbies outside their fields. On the other hand, if you truly enjoy learning about life's inner workings, then you'll get paid to have fun! "You're always a student," says Mason, "and the universe is your hobby."

accomplishments rather than job descriptions. List specific technical skills you've acquired. Don't neglect "soft skills," or the social aptitudes that employers want to see, such as a strong work ethic, teamwork, the ability to work independently, and a positive attitude. Fold skills into experience when possible, showing which of your talents you applied to each job or accomplishment.

COVER LETTERS

Like your résumé, your cover letter needs to be written specifically for the employer you're sending it to. You want to explain why you're the best choice for the job. This is partially about how your skills and experience match the employer's needs, but it also covers why you want to work for that employer. Who'll want to hire you for a job you're not really interested in, one that you're planning on moving on from as soon as something better comes along? You need to explain what it is about the job and the employer that excites you. This will involve research. Know the history and methods of the hiring company or institution, learn what projects you might be involved in, and research any renowned scientists on the team that you'd be working with.

Always return calls and e-mails promptly, with the same care and precision you take for more formal communications, like your résumé and cover letter. You want the hiring manager to think you're reliable, not a slacker.

INTERVIEW R&D

Arrive on time for your interview. Too early is almost as bad as too late! Be honest and confident. Do your homework on the hiring company or department and on the current state of the industry. You want to ask questions that make you look sharp and interested, not ignorant. You'll also want to look into whether the company is doing poorly or its culture doesn't suit you, since a hiring manager may not be up front about such things. You'll need to know what salaries in the industry look like when the hiring manager asks for your salary expectations. Follow up with the hiring manager on a regular basis afterward.

Remember that even if the job market is strong at the moment in your area, you can't count on getting hired quickly or easily. Don't put all your eggs in one basket. Apply for multiple jobs and keep applying for new ones even while you're in the interview process. Make as much use of professional contacts as possible. Ask friends and acquaintances in the industry, including your professors, to speak on your behalf to potential employers. More important, expand your network of contacts by attending networking events and professional conferences in your field. You can

In a job interview, it's important to show that you're confident, knowledgeable about the field, and interested in the specific company with which you're seeking employment.

also ask your existing contacts to introduce you to other biotechnologists. Your network can never be too big—70 percent of all jobs are found by networking!

Continuing education is a powerful tool for carving out a place in the industry, whether to get promoted, to find a better job, or to find a new position after you're laid off. This is especially important in fast-moving fields like biotechnology, where you'll need to keep abreast of new discoveries and practices simply to keep performing your current job effectively. Look into evening classes at local colleges or online courses of study from accredited websites. Attend professional conferences and on-the-job training seminars. Talk to your human resources department to see if your employer will pay for continuing education outside the workplace.

YOUR SECURITY CLEARANCE BEGINS NOW

Some of the highest-paying and most interesting jobs related to biotechnology, both in the public and private sectors, may require a government security clearance. While this can lead you down remarkable paths, such as counterterrorism work, it also encompasses many otherwise-mundane biotech careers. The federal government can classify data as secret and employees must possess a security clearance to work with such data. Such jobs are either for the federal government or for a federal contractor—a private company that's being paid by the federal government to supply goods or services.

Even outside of the government sphere, employers see a security clearance as an important job qualification. Those who possess a security clearance earn significantly more than their uncleared peers—10 percent more for engineers, for example.

However, getting a security clearance is a time-consuming process—the security questionnaire is over a hundred pages long, and it can take months for your

Passing a security check involves lots of time and extensive documentation. Though arduous, it can pay off down the line by opening up more interesting and higher-paying jobs.

application to be processed. You'll need to answer a lot of questions, undergo a background check, and submit to an interview. You'll be subject to a follow-up investigation every five years.

In any case, you can't simply apply for a security clearance on your own. A potential employer has to sponsor you when you apply for a job that requires clearance.

Things that can result in your application being denied include, but are not limited to, a pattern of criminal behavior or rule-breaking in the workplace; self-destructive activity, such as illegal drug use, alcohol abuse, or high-risk sexual activity; major, chronic financial problems; untreated mental health issues; or lying in the clearance investigation.

The main disadvantage to cleared work is secrecy. You won't be permitted to talk about your work. You'll have to follow elaborate security procedures in the workplace to keep information—whether it's e-mail, flash drives, or hardcopy—from getting out.

CHAPTER SEVEN

THE FUTURE OF BIOTECHNOLOGY

As wild and exciting as today's cutting-edge biotech may be, there's even crazier stuff on the horizon. Some of it is in the early stages of development now. Other projects, though merely hypothetical, are nonetheless breathlessly anticipated by futurists who're aiming to give shape to the impossible.

BIOTECH ON THE DRAWING BOARD

Any number of new transgenic organisms are under development. For example, researchers at Utah State University are working with "spider goats"—goats that

These are transgenic rice plants. Biotechnologists have genetically altered rice—a staple crop for half the world—to resist pests and increase yields.

have been genetically modified to produce spider silk proteins in their milk. The scientists are working to figure out a cost-effective method of transforming the proteins into incredibly strong, resilient, lightweight synthetic fibers, usable for purposes as diverse as bulletproof vests and ligament repair.

Food scientists have developed an enzyme treatment for peanuts that breaks down the allergens responsible for potentially fatal peanut allergies, which afflict millions of people. Similar treatments should soon be under development for other allergenic foods.

Biomedical scientists are approaching the problem of bleeding wounds from multiple directions. There are now tourniquets that use ultrasound to cause clotting in damaged blood vessels in perhaps as little as 30 seconds. Scientists have also developed "liquid bandages" that seal damaged blood vessels on contact and eventually biodegrade so they don't need to be cleaned out of the wound.

More dramatic, researchers are now creating replacement human body parts by growing stem cells on pre-shaped polymer templates, creating a variety of organs—ears, noses, blood vessels, and more—that can be transplanted into the DNA donor. These would have enormous advantages over normal transplants. Since they'd share the donor's genes, the donor's immune system wouldn't consider them foreign, removing the risk of rejection. Procedures to clone more complex organs, such as kidneys and lungs, are under development. Meanwhile, experiments in rats have had some success in using stem cells to repair brain damage left by stroke.

Gene therapy has also shown success in the lab. To avoid the problems that come with implanting an artificial pacemaker to cope with an irregular heartbeat, geneticists are working on a therapeutic virus that would alter heart cells to restore the heart's natural pacemaking function. It has already been tested successfully on pigs, whose heartbeat improved in just one day. Therapeutic viruses to cure such disorders as diabetes and hemophilia outright have been successfully tested on dogs, eliminating all symptoms after just a single treatment.

FREEZING TIME

Today's scientists are experimenting with various ways to use freezing technology. Cryonics is the process of freezing human bodies in hopes that they can be revived and repaired in the future. As of yet cryonics has shown no sign of being a successful way to sidestep death.

However, researchers are testing short-term suspended animation as a means to keep people alive long enough to treat traumatic injuries. All the blood in a patient's body is replaced with a saline solution at temperatures that are low enough to prevent brain damage. After successful pig trials, human testing is in the works.

BIOETHICS: PLAYING GOD

There are so many moral and ethical questions and controversies surrounding genetic engineering, life extension, and other biotechnologies that these questions form their own field of study: bioethics. Anyone interested in the field should take the time to consider the positive and negative aspects of biotechnology. These range from the abstract—how will life extension affect civilization a thousand years in the future?—to the immediate effects of a newly released technology or genetically modified organism on our lives and our environment. These risks and threats must be balanced against the real and potential benefits of biotechnology, such as saving lives and increasing quality of life.

Given the impact that biotechnology has on society and the environment, it's important to discuss and debate the potential consequences of biotech innovations.

Like so much else in life, a lot of bioethical questions revolve around money. The fruits of technological research—from biometric security to cancer treatments—always start out expensive and can remain so if the resources or skills involved are hard to come by. When medical advances are too expensive for the average person to take advantage of, only the wealthy can reap the benefits. This effect could be exaggerated by biotechnology, as wealthy recipients will be the main beneficiaries

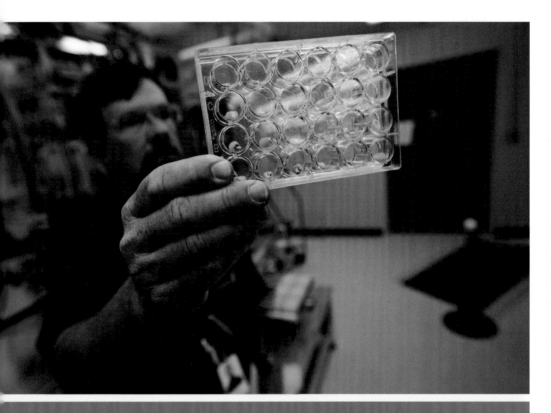

A scientist at agribusiness conglomerate Monsanto examines a grid of genetically modified (GM) seeds. The ethics of GM products, such as patented genomes and sterile "terminator" seeds, is hotly debated.

of extended health and long life, giving them more time to make themselves and their families richer. How do we achieve a fair distribution of life-improving technology in a society with an uneven distribution of wealth?

On a related note, biological patents on genetic material and genetically modified organisms have the potential to be exploited. The U.S. Supreme Court has banned patents on the human genome, but other biological material remains patentable, with mixed results. Witness the controversy over sterile "terminator seeds" and the legal complications from GMO pollen contaminating neighboring crops or honey production. Biological patents are said to encourage businesses to invest money in biotechnology research, but they also limit research and development by restricting access to those genes, especially when the patented genes occur in nature.

Biorisk is the possibility that genetically modified organisms will cause direct or indirect harm to humanity. This might take the form of actively dangerous microorganisms that attack humans or some key part of the food chain, or by contaminating crops or livestock by inadvertently spreading modified genes throughout the population. Biorisk also includes the possibility of deliberately unleashing such dangers in the form of bioterrorism or biological warfare.

BIOTECH IN THE MINDS OF FUTURISTS

For all of the practical uses to which researchers are putting stem cells, other uses currently remain theoretical.

One of these—for which we've seen partial success in mouse testing—is the prospect of turning stem cells into sperm or egg cells. If developed, such technology would allow infertile or same-gender couples to have children that share their genes.

One prong of anti-cancer research deals with onco-lytic viruses. These are viruses that have been modified and tailored to attack cancer cells without harming healthy cells. Oncolytics has shown limited success in both animal testing and human clinical trials—not enough for a genuine oncolytic therapy to be in development, but more than effective enough to encourage microbiologists and geneticists to pursue it as a path to destroying malignant tumors.

For those concerned about animal welfare, in vitro meat—that is, meat that's grown in a lab from cell cultures—is bound to be of interest. Unfortunately, efforts in this field are currently prohibitively expensive, with a single in vitro hamburger costing $325,000 to manufacture and cultured in an unkind-to-animals serum made from fetal calves. Nonetheless, some scientists hope to eventually make lab-grown meat an affordable, ethical alternative to slaughtering livestock. (Synthetic milk has proven far easier to manufacture; food scientists are currently using genetically modified yeast that contains cow DNA to produce lactose-free milk in the lab.)

Even animals that have completely died out may yet be revived by genetic modification. Researchers in the "de-extinction" movement have been sequencing the genomes of specimens of extinct species, such as the Tasmanian tiger, the great auk, and the passenger pigeon, in hopes of cloning new specimens, Jurassic

Park–style. If the passenger pigeons return, they may find the once all-but-extinct American chestnut that formed their food source and habitat—now rendered immune to chestnut blight through implantation of wheat genes—revived and waiting for them.

One of the ultimate goals of medical researchers is indefinite life extension, defeating the aging process. This requires dealing with the genetic and metabolic root causes of aging, while avoiding the overcompensation

Extinct for close to a century, the Tasmanian tiger, or thylacine, is one of many animals that scientists in the "de-extinction" movement hope to revive through genetic engineering.

that leads to cancer—itself a form of cellular immortality. Researchers are currently focused on a seemingly ageless jellyfish species, *Turritopsis nutricula*, which can repeatedly return to a juvenile state in order to recover from injury.

Some thinkers propose even more radical changes and improvements to human bodies and minds. Transhumanism is the philosophy that humanity should surpass its current limitations through technology. Proposed advancements include bionic or genetic enhancement of physical strength, intelligence, or memory; establishing direct links between the human mind and computers; or even treating the mind as data that can be mapped and copied onto computer networks—currently a matter of science fiction. Ethicists debate the appropriateness of such changes and the personhood of those who might undergo extensive transhuman modification.

GLOSSARY

assay A chemical test for a specific quality or substance. In biotechnology, this usually means a test to find whether a specific organic molecule is present in a sample or specimen.

biofuels Man-made fuels created from organic matter, such as vegetable oil or wood pulp.

bioinformatics The science of using computers to gather, analyze, and manage biological data such as genetic information.

bioreactor A container in which biological transformations, such as fermentation or enzyme-based transformations, take place.

clinical trial A test of a drug or medical device on human volunteers to ensure that it's both safe and effective.

electrophoresis The use of an electrical field to separate things—usually molecules, such as DNA or proteins—into separate groups based on size and electrical charge.

enzyme A molecule, typically a protein, that speeds up chemical reactions, such as connecting or breaking down other molecules, without being affected itself.

fermentation The process by which microorganisms break down carbohydrates into smaller molecules.

gene therapy A process for preventing or treating genetic disorders by changing the genes that trigger those disorders.

genetic engineering The process of modifying the genetic code in the cells of living creatures to change their traits.

genome The complete DNA structure of all of a living creature's genes.

GMO A living creature whose genetic code has been artificially changed. GMO is short for genetically modified organism.

graft A portion of bodily tissue—such as a piece of skin or a blood vessel—that has been transplanted from one part of the body to another, or from one person to another.

life sciences A category containing all those fields of scientific study that deal with living things, such as biology, biochemistry, genetics, and medicine.

medical device Any technological item used in the diagnosis, treatment, or prevention of disease or injury. These range from humble tongue depressors and stethoscopes to sophisticated medical implants, scanners, and prostheses.

prosthetic An artificial body part, such as a limb or organ, that replaces a damaged or missing part.

reagent A chemical that is added to other substances to cause a chemical reaction. Often used to test for the presence of a specific molecule or substance.

sequencing Discovering the unique pattern of building blocks in a piece of DNA or RNA.

stem cells Cells in the body that can divide to make more cells, creating either more stem cells or cells of other types, such as blood cells or muscle tissue. Some are found in bone marrow or other bodily organs, others in embryos.

transgenic Having to do with a plant or animal that has been altered to contain DNA from another species.

FOR MORE INFORMATION

BioEd Online
Center for Educational Outreach
Baylor College of Medicine
One Baylor Plaza, BCM411
Houston, TX 77030
(713) 798-8200 or (800) 798-8244
Website: http://www.bioedonline.org
An online resource for science teachers, BioEd Online
    provides a broad range of educational materials
    on life science topics, including lessons, slideshows,
    and downloadable books.

Bio-Link
1855 Folsom Street, Suite 643
San Francisco, CA 94103
(415) 487-2470
Website: http://www.bio-link.org
Bio-Link partners with high schools across the country to
    provide educational resources for students and teach-
    ers alike. Its site also offers information on schools,
    employers, and careers in the biotech sector.

BioSpace
6465 South Greenwood Plaza, Suite 400
Centennial, CO 80111
(877) 277-7585
Website: http://www.biospace.com
A privately owned company, BioSpace offers biotech-
    nology news and career opportunities, including

book reviews, job fairs, and information on companies in the field.

BioTalent Canada
300-130 Slater Street
Ottawa, ON K1P 6E2
Canada
(613) 235-1402
Website: https://biotalent.ca
BioTalent Canada is a nonprofit employment resource
    for the Canadian biotech industry. It offers a range
    of career tools, such as skill profiles for various
    occupations, a résumé builder, and a job board.

BIOTECanada
1 Nicholas Street, Suite 600
Ottawa, ON K1N 7B7
Canada
(613) 230-5585
Website: http://www.biotech.ca/en/default.aspx
BIOTECanada is Canada's national association for
    the biotech industry. Resources include educational
    PDFs, corporate press releases, and links to Canadi-
    an and international biotech blogs.

Biotechnology Industry Organization (BIO)
1201 Maryland Avenue SW, Suite 900
Washington, DC 20024
(202) 962-9200
Website: http://www.bio.org
BIO is the world's largest biotech trade organization,
    providing advocacy for businesses, universities,
    and other public and private organizations. Though

aimed primarily at employers, BIO maintains a job board for those seeking employment in the field.

National Center for Biotechnology Information
National Library of Medicine, Building 38A
Bethesda, MD 20894
Website: http://www.ncbi.nlm.nih.gov
The National Center for Biotechnology Information offers databases, gene maps, and other high-level information, tools, and tutorials for researchers and college students involved in biomedicine.

Society for Industrial Microbiology and
    Biotechnology (SIMB)
3929 Old Lee Highway, Suite 92A
Fairfax, VA 22030
(703) 691-3357
Website: http://www.simbhq.org
This international nonprofit is dedicated to furthering the science of microbiology and its biotechnology applications. Members receive subscriptions to industry magazines, discounts on biotech courses and other services, and access to the SIMB career center.

WEBSITES

Because of the changing nature of Internet links, Rosen Publishing has developed an online list of websites related to the subject of this book. This site is updated regularly. Please use this link to access the list:

http://www.rosenlinks.com/PTC/Bio

FOR FURTHER READING

Allen, Robert, ed. *Bulletproof Feathers: How Science Uses Nature's Secrets to Design Cutting-Edge Technology.* Chicago, IL: University of Chicago Press, 2010.

Anthes, Emily. *Frankenstein's Cat: Cuddling Up to Biotech's Brave New Beasts.* New York, NY: Farrar, Straus and Giroux, 2013.

Bacigalupi, Paolo. *The Windup Girl.* New York, NY: Start Publishing, 2009.

Bradley, James T. *Brutes or Angels: Human Possibility in the Age of Biotechnology.* Tuscaloosa, AL: University of Alabama Press, 2013.

Cannon, Zander, and Kevin Cannon. *The Stuff of Life: A Graphic Guide to Genetics and DNA.* New York, NY: Hill and Wang, 2009.

Chorost, Michael. *World Wide Mind: The Coming Integration of Humanity, Machines, and the Internet.* New York, NY: Free Press, 2011.

Church, George M., and Ed Regis. *Regenesis: How Synthetic Biology Will Reinvent Nature and Ourselves.* New York, NY: Basic Books, 2012.

Collins, Francis S. *The Language of Life: DNA and the Revolution in Personalized Medicine.* New York, NY: HarperCollins Publishers, 2013.

Denison, R. Ford. *Darwinian Agriculture: How Understanding Evolution Can Improve Agriculture.* Princeton, NJ: Princeton University Press, 2012.

Firestein, Stuart. *Ignorance: How It Drives Science.* Chicago, IL: University of Chicago Press, 2012.

Freedman, Jeri. *Genetically Modified Food: How Biotechnology Is Changing What We Eat.* New York, NY: Rosen Publishing, 2009.

Freedman, Toby. *Career Opportunities in Biotechnology and Drug Development.* Cold Spring Harbor, NY: Cold Spring Harbor Laboratory Press, 2009.

Goodsell, David S. *The Machinery of Life.* Göttingen, Germany: Copernicus Publications, 2010.

Hughes, Sally Smith. *Genentech: The Beginnings of Biotech.* Chicago, IL: University of Chicago Press, 2011.

Kurpinski, Kyle, and Terry D. Johnson. *How to Defeat Your Own Clone and Other Tips for Surviving the Biotech Revolution.* New York, NY: Bantam Books, 2009.

Lewis, Ricki. *The Forever Fix: Gene Therapy and the Boy Who Saved It.* New York, NY: St. Martin's Griffin, 2013.

Madhavan, Guruprasad, Barbara Oakley, and Luis Kun, eds. *Career Development in Bioengineering and Biotechnology.* Berlin, Germany: Springer Science + Business Media, 2008.

Pearson, Mary E. *The Adoration of Jenna Fox.* New York, NY: Square Fish Books, 2008.

Rutherford, Adam. *Creation: How Science Is Reinventing Life Itself.* New York, NY: Penguin Group, 2013.

Stockwell, Brent R. *The Quest for the Cure: The Science and Stories Behind the Next Generation of Medicines.* New York, NY: Columbia University Press, 2013.

BIBLIOGRAPHY

Bains, William. *Biotechnology from A to Z.* Third ed. New York, NY: Oxford University Press, 2004.

Beale, Renee. "Mathematics Is the Key to Science Success." *Science Matters*, February 1, 2010. Retrieved October 21, 2014 (http://sciencematters .unimelb.edu.au/2010/02/mathematics-is-the-key -to-science-success).

Bureau of Labor Statistics. *Occupational Outlook Handbook.* Retrieved October 21, 2014 (http://www .bls.gov/ooh/home.htm).

Cornell University. "Networking Made Easy." Retrieved October 21, 2014 (http://as.cornell.edu/ academics/careers/networking/).

Grant, Kelli B. "How Much Will College Cost in 25 Years?" CNBC, September 10, 2014. Retrieved October 21, 2014 (http://www.cnbc.com/id/ 101971996).

Jackson, Alex. "Our Furry Friends Now Are Shaped by Biotechnology." *Scientific American*, April 10, 2014. Retrieved October 21, 2014 (http://www .scientificamerican.com/article/our-furry-friends -now-are-shaped-by-biotechnology).

Kong, Nikki R. "Chasing Immortality." *Berkeley Science Review*, April 22, 2013. Retrieved October 21, 2014 (http://berkeleysciencereview.com/ article/chasing-immortality).

Mayo Clinic. "Personalized Medicine and Pharmacogenomics." Retrieved October 21, 2014 (http:// www.mayoclinic.org).

Medgadget. Retrieved October 21, 2014 (http://www.medgadget.com).

Medical Daily. Retrieved October 21, 2014 (http://www.medicaldaily.com).

Medical News Today. Retrieved October 21, 2014 (http://www.medicalnewstoday.com).

Mother Nature Network. "12 Bizarre Examples of Genetic Engineering." 2010. Retrieved October 21, 2014 (http://www.mnn.com).

New Scientist. Retrieved October 21, 2014 (http://www.newscientist.com).

Science Buddies. "Careers in Science." Retrieved October 21, 2014 (http://www.sciencebuddies.org/science-engineering-careers).

Science Daily. Retrieved October 21, 2014 (http://www.sciencedaily.com).

U.S. Department of State. "Security Clearances: FAQs." Retrieved October 21, 2014 (http://www.state.gov/m/ds/clearances/c10977.htm).

Wohlsen, Marcus. *Biopunk: Solving Biotech's Biggest Problems in Kitchens and Garages*. New York, NY: Penguin Group, 2012.

INDEX

ABOUT THE AUTHOR

Eric Minton is a writer and journalist living in New York City. He has worked on a number of health and medicine publications, including *POZ, AIDSmeds, Hep,* and *Sane.* As a voracious reader and published author of science fiction, he has had a longtime interest in biotechnology and futurism. In addition to writing *Powering Up a Career in Biotechnology*, he has also written five children's books on the safe use of online technology.

PHOTO CREDITS

Cover Milles Studio/Shutterstock.com; cover (background), back cover, p. 1 Sofiaworld/Shutterstock.com; p. 5 Jaco Wolmarans/E+/ Getty Images; pp. 9, 45 BSIP/UIG/Getty Images; p. 10 Vin Catania/ AFP/Getty Images; p. 13 The Lighthouse/Science Source; p. 15 © iStockphoto.com/Steve Debenport; pp. 17, 27 Monty Rakusen/ Cultura/Getty Images; p. 21 Ute Grabowsky/Photothek/Getty Images; p. 23 Roy Mehta/Iconica/Getty Images; p. 28 Javier Larrea/ age fotostock/Getty Images; p. 32 Frank Perry/AFP/Getty Images; p. 34 Huntstock/Getty Images; p. 35 Morsa Images/Digital Vision/ Getty Images; p. 38 chinaface/E+/Getty Images; p. 42 © Cultura/ ZUMA Wire; p. 46 Juan Mabromata/AFP/Getty Images; p. 50 Bloomberg/Getty Images; p. 51 lightpoet/Shutterstock.com; p. 55 pan_kung/Shutterstock.com; p. 57 Ariel Skelley/Blend Images/ Getty Images; p. 59 Pascal Goetgheluck/Science Source; pp. 62–63 M_a_y_a/E+/Getty Images; p. 64 Brent Stirton/Getty Images; p. 67 Torsten Blackwood/AFP/Getty Images; cover and interior pages design elements Zffoto/Shutterstock.com, Sergey Nivens/ Shutterstock.com, elen_studio/Shutterstock.com, Lukas Rs/Shutterstock .com, Nucleartist/Shutterstock.com, Georg Preissl/Shutterstock.com, Jack1e/Shutterstock.com, Sfio Cracho/Shutterstock.com.

Designer: Michael Moy; Editor: Amelie von Zumbusch